INTRODUCTION

TO

CO-ORDINATION CHEMISTRY

Dr SAPANA GUPTA

Assistant Professor
Department of Chemistry
Seth Phollchand Agrawal College Nawapara Raipur CG

&

Dr. Vinod Jena

Assistant Professor
Department of Chemistry
Govt College Sarona Kanker CG India

2015

First Printing: 2015

ISBN: 978-1-312-87695-8

Dedication

To my friends all over the world
Thank you all.
Without your support and patience, I would have
never achieved my dream

Preface

Coordination chemistry is a fascinating field in inorganic chemistry. Coordination compounds are of great practical importance. This book is written with the assumption that readers will have completed an introductory tertiary-level course in general chemistry or its equivalent, and thus be familiar with theories of chemical concepts including the foundations of coordination compounds chemistry. This allows those who are not intending to specialize in the field or who simply wish to supplement their own separate area of expertise to gain a good understanding largely free of a heavy theoretical loading. While not seeking to diminish aspects that are both important and central to higher-level understanding, this is a pragmatic approach towards what is, after all, an introductory text. In the present handbook it has been attempted to offer an easy approach to understand the different theories of coordination chemistry.

SAPANA GUPTA
Raipur India

INTRODUCTION

TO

CO-ORDINATION CHEMISTRY

Contents

Chapter 1

Naming Coordination Compounds

A complex is a substance in which a metal atom or ion is associated with a group of neutral molecules or anions called ligands. Coordination compounds are neutral substances (i.e. uncharged) in which at least one ion is present as a complex.

Nomenclature of Coordination Complexes

Rule 1:

The names of neutral coordination complexes are given without spaces. For coordination compounds that are ionic (i.e., the coordination complex is either an anion or anion of an ionic substance), the cation is named first and separated by a space from the anion, as is the case for all ionic compounds.

$K_2[CuBr_4]$

Potassium tetrabromocuprate(II)

In the above examples, the cations sodium and potassium are named first and then

separated by a space from the names of the anions.

$trans$-$[Co(en)_2I(H_2O)](NO_3)_2$

$trans$-Aquabis(ethylenediamine)iodocobalt(III) nitrate

In this example the coordination cation is written without spaces and then separated from

the name of the anion.

mer-$[Ru(PPh_3)_3Cl_3]$

mer-trichlorotris(triphenylphosphine)ruthenium(III)

Here the coordination complex is neutral, so no spaces are necessary.

Rule 2:

The name of the coordination compound (neutral, cationic or anionic) begins with the names of the ligands. The metal is listed next, following in parentheses by the oxidation state of the metal.

Rule 3:

When more than one of a given ligand is bound to the same metal atom or ion, the number of such ligands is designated by the following prefixes

2 di 6 hexa 10 deca
2 tri 7 hepta 11 undeca
4 tetra 8 octa 12 dodeca
5 penta 9 nona

However, when the name of the ligand in question already contains one of these prefixes

(generally ligand names that are three syllables or longer), then a prefix from the
following list is used instead:
2 bis 6 hexakis
3 tris 7 heptakis
4 tetrakis 8 octakis
5 pentakis 9 ennea

Rule 4:

Neutral ligands are given the same name as the uncoordinated molecule, but with
spaces omitted. Some examples are:

$(CH_3)_3SO$ dimethylsulfoxide (DMSO)

$(NH_2)_2CO$ urea

C_5H_5N pyridine

terpy terpyridine

bpy 2,2'-bipyridine

en ethylenediamine

PCl$_3$ trichlorophosphine

PPh$_3$ triphenylphopshine

EXCEPTIONS: Some neutral molecules, when serving as ligands are given special

names. These are:

NH$_3$ ammine

H$_2$O aqua

NO nitrosyl

CO carbonyl

CS thiocarbonyl

Rule 5:

Anionic ligands are given names that end in the letter "o". When the name of the free, uncoordinated anion ends in "ate", the ligand name is changed to end in "ato".

Some examples are :

CH$_3$CO$_2$

- (acetate) acetato

SO$_4^{2-}$ (sulfate) sulfato

CO$_3^{2-}$ (carbonate) carbonato

 acac acetylacetonato

When the name of the free, uncoordinated anion ends in "ide", the ligand name is

changed to end in "ido". Some examples are:

N^{3-} (nitride) nitrido

4

N_3- (azide) azido

NH_2- (amide) amido

$(CH_3)_2N$- (dimethylamide) dimethylamido

When the name of the free, uncoordinated anion ends in "ite", the ligand name is changed

to end in "ito". Some examples are:

NO_2- (nitrite) nitrito

$SO_3{}^{2-}$ (sulfite) sulfido

ClO_3- (chlorite) chlorito

Certain anionic ligands are given special names, all ending in "o":

CN^-	Cyno
C^-	Chloro
Br^-	Bromo
F^-	Fluoro
I^-	Iodo
O^{2-}	Oxo
$OH-$	Hydroxo
$H-$	Hydrido
CH_3O-	methoxo

Rule 6:

The ligands are named alphabetically, ignoring the prefixes *bis*, *tris*, etc...

Rule 7:

When the coordination entity is either neutral or cationic, the usual name of the metal is used, followed in parentheses by the oxidation state of the metal. However, when the coordination entity is an anion, the name of the metal is altered to end in "ate". This is done for some metals by simply changing the ending "ium" to "ate":

Scandium scandate

Titanium titanate

Chromium chromate

Zirconium zirconate

Niobium niobate

Ruthenium ruthenate

For other metals, the name is given the ending "ate":

Manganese manganate

Cobalt cobaltate

Nickel nickelate

Tantalum tantalate

Tungsten tungstate

Palladium palladate

Rhenium rhenate

Platinum Platinate

Finally the name of some metals are based on Latin name of the element

Iron Ferrate

Copper Cuprate

Silver Argentate

Cold Aurate

Rule 8:

Optical isomers are designated by the symbols (+) or (-). Geometrical isomers are designated by *cis-* or *trans-* and *mer-* or *fac-*, the latter two standing for meridional or facial, respectively.

Rule 9: Bridging ligands are designated with the prefix μ-. When there are two bridging ligands of the same kind, the prefix di- μ- is used. Bridging ligands are listed in order with other ligands, according to Rule 6, and set off between hypens. An important exception arises when the molecule is symmetrical, and a more compact name can be given by listing the bridging ligand first.

Rule 9 is illustrated in the following examples:

Pentamminecobalt(III)-?-amidotetraamineaquacobalt(III) chloride

Tetraamminecobalt(III)-?-amido-?-superoxotetraamminecobalt(III)

The bridging $-O_2-$ group in the above example is named form the superoxide anion O_2-, because the physical data suggest the -1 charge

8

?-Hydroxobis[pentaamminechromium(III)] bromide

Di-?-chloro-bis[diammineplatinum(II)] chloride

Rule 10: Ligands that are capable of linkage isomerism are given specific names for each mode of attachment.

-SCN⁻	thiocyanato (S-thiocyanato)
-NCS⁻	isothiocyanto (N-thiocyanto)
-NCSe⁻	isoselenocyanato (N-selenocyanato)
-NO₂⁻	nitro
-ONO⁻	nitrito

Examples

$$[Co(NH_3)_5CO_3]Cl$$
Pentaamminecarbonatocobalt(III) chloride

$$[Cr(H_2O)_4Cl_2]Cl$$
Tetraaquadichlorochromium(III) chloride

$$K_2[OsCl_5N]$$
Potassium pentachloronitridoosmate(VI)

$$K_3[Fe(CN)_5NO]$$
Potassium pentacyanonitrosylferrate(II)

Structures of Common Chelating Ligands

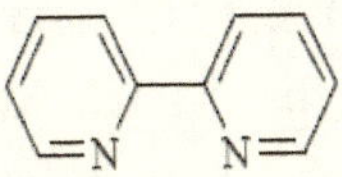

2,2'-bipyridine (bpy)

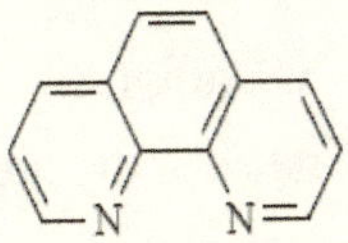

1,10-phenanthroline (phen)

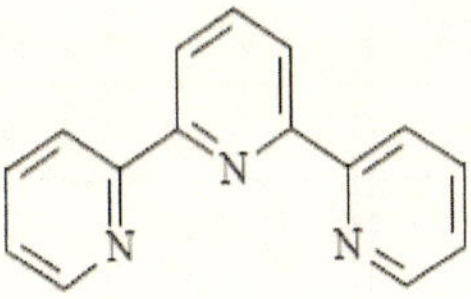

terpyridine (terpy)

ethylenediamine (en)

propylenediamine (pn)

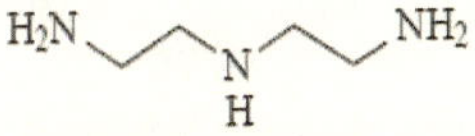

diethylenetriamine (dien)

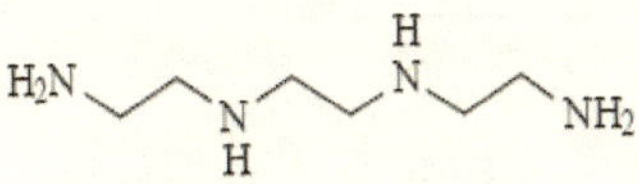

triethylenetetramine (trien)

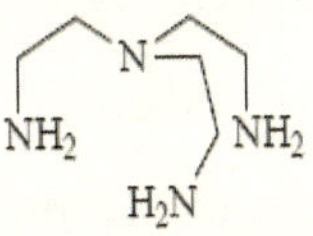

tri(ethylenediamine)amine (tren)

Nomenclature of Coordination Compounds:

Lewis bases may be anions, molecules, or (rarely) cations and are called 'ligands'. The donor atom is the atom of the ligand, which actually donates the electrons (underlined in the table). [* = bidentate ligands]

formula	name	ligand name	formula	name	ligand name
:$\underline{N}H_3$	ammonia	ammine	$\underline{Cl}^-$	chloride	chloro
$H_2\underline{O}$	water	aqua	$\underline{F}^-$	fluoride	fluoro
:$\underline{C}\equiv O$:	carbon monoxide	carbonyl	:$\underline{C}\equiv N$:$^-$	cyanide	cyano
:$\underline{P}H_3$	phosphine	phosphine	$\underline{O}H^-$	hydroxide	hydroxo
:$\underline{N}=O$	nitric oxide	nitrosyl	:$\underline{N}O_2^-$	nitrite	nitro (NO_2^-)
$\underline{N}O_3^-$	nitrate	nitrato	:$N\underline{O}_2^-$	nitrite	nitrito (ONO^-)
$\underline{N}H_2^-$	amide	amido	*$S\underline{O}_4^{-2}$	sulfate	sulfato
*$C_2\underline{O}_4^{-2}$	oxalate	oxalato	$SC\underline{N}^-$	thiocyanate	thiocyanato
*$C\underline{O}_3^{-2}$	carbonate	carbonato	*$S_2\underline{O}_3^{-2}$	thiosulfate	thiosulfato
*$\underline{O}^{-2}$	oxide	oxo	$C_5H_5\underline{N}$:	pyridine	pyridine

Coordination number of a metal is the number of donor atoms to which the metal is bonded. If the ligands are unidentate, then the coordination number is also the number of ligands. For example, in $[Co(en)_3]^{+3}$ where each ethylenediamine ligand is bidentate, the coordination number is 6, i.e., Co^{+3} is bonded to 6 donor atoms (2 donor atoms from each of 3 ethylenediamine ligands).

Coordination sphere is the metal and its ligands but not the uncoordinated counterions, e.g., in $[Co(NH_3)_6]Cl_3$, the coordination sphere = $[Co(NH_3)_6]^{+3}$.

12

Examples: Give the systematic names for the following coordination compounds:

1. $[Cr(NH_3)_3(H_2O)_3]Cl_3$

Answer: triamminetriaquachromium(III) chloride

2. $[Pt(NH_3)_5Cl]Br_3$

Answer: pentaamminechloroplatinum(IV) bromide

3. $[Pt(H_2NCH_2CH_2NH_2)_2Cl_2]Cl_2$

Answer: dichlorobis(ethylenediamine)platinum(IV) chloride

4. $[Co(H_2NCH_2CH_2NH_2)_3]_2(SO_4)_3$

Answer: tris(ethylenediamine)cobalt(III) sulfate

5. $K_4[Fe(CN)_6]$

Answer: potassium hexacyanoferrate(II)

6. $Na_2[NiCl_4]$

Answer: sodium tetrachloronickelate(II)

7. $Pt(NH_3)_2Cl_4$

Answer: diamminetetrachloroplatinum(IV)

9. $(NH_4)_2[Ni(C_2O_4)_2(H_2O)_2]$

Answer: ammonium diaquabis(oxalato)nickelate(II)

10. $[Ag(NH_3)_2][Ag(CN)$

Answer: diamminesilver(I) dicyanoargentate(I)

11. $Na [PtCl3(NH3)]$

Sodium amminetrichloroplatinate(II)

12. $K2[CuBr4]$

Potassium tetrabromocuprate(II)

Postulates of Werner's Theory of Coordination Compounds

- In coordination compounds, there are two types of linkages (valences) – primary and secondary.

- The primary valences are ionisable, and are satisfied by negative ions.

- The secondary valences are non-ionisable, and are satisfied by negative ions or neutral molecules.

- Primary valence is known as oxidation number of central metal ion while secondary valence is equal to the coordination number of a metal, and remains fixed for a metal.

- Secondary valence indicates geometry of the complexes.

- The primary valence is non-directional. The secondary valence is directional. Ions or molecules attached to satisfy secondary valences have characteristic spatial arrangements. Secondary valence decides geometry of the complex compound.

What are the limitations of Werner's theory of coordination compounds

This theory fails to explain why,

a) A few elements have the property to form coordination compounds

b) The bonds in coordination compounds have directional properties

c) Coordination compounds have characteristic magnetic and optical properties.

Chapter 2

Study of Valance Bond Theory

Main assumptions of VBT

- The central metal in complex makes available empty orbital for M-L bonding.
- The number of empty orbital is equal to Coordination number of of the central metal.
- The appropriate atomic orbitals (s, p , d, etc) of the metal hybridize to give a set of equivalent orbitals of definite geometry i.e. Sp, Td, Oh, etc.
- The d-orbital involvd in hybridization may be either inner i.e.(n-1)d or outer i.e. nd.
- Each ligand has at least one orbital containing lone pair of electrons.
- The empty hybrid orbitals of metal ion overlap with the filled orbital of the ligand to form M-L coordinate bonds.

Structures of Coordination Compounds

Coordination number 3

The most symmetrical 3 coordinate arrangements are planar (having D3hgeometry) and pyramidal (having C3vgeometry). This coordination number is rare for metal complexes, because nearly all MX3metal complexes have structures where sharing of ligands leads to a higher coordination number for metal. A few exceptions are known, including the MN3group that occur in Cr/Fe(NR2)3.

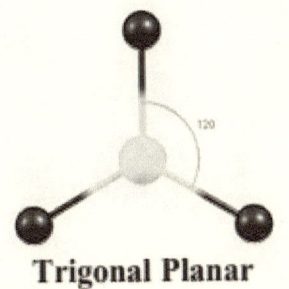
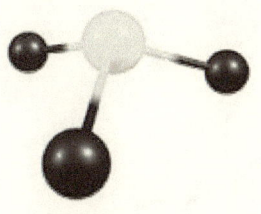

Trigonal Planar   **Trigonal Pyramid**

Coordination number 4

There are three principal geometries for 4-coordinate complexes; the tetrahedral geometry (with symmetry T_d), the square planar geometry (with symmetry D_{4h}) and the irregular arrangement of symmetry that may occur whena ligand in a trigonal bipyramidal (TBP) arrangement is replaced by a lone pair of electrons. The square planar arrangement typically occurs in many transition metal complexes because of the presence of additional valence shell electrons. A substitution of one of the ligands in a tetrahedral geometry typically gives pseudotetrahedral arrangements with local symmetry C_{3v} about the metal ion

 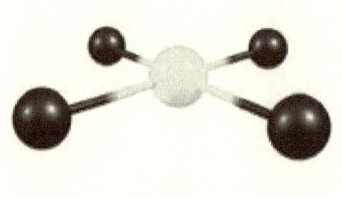

Trigonal Pyramid   **Square Planar**

Coordination number 5

For 5-coordinate complexes, there are two principal geometries; the trigonal bipyramidal (TBP) arrangement (having D_{3h} symmetry) and the square pyramidal (SQP) arrangement (having C_{4v} symmetry). For the TBP arrangement, a substitution of one of the axial ligands typically would lower the symmetry to C3vwhereas a substitution of one of the equatorial ligands would lower the symmetry to C_{2v}. Pentagonal planar coordination, where two ligands are bidentate and one monodentate, is very unusual and seems to be due to the presence of two stereochemically active lone pairs.

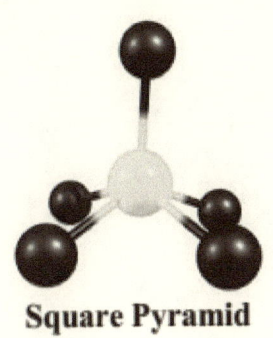 

Square Pyramid **Trigonal Bipyramid**

Coordination number 6

There are three principal forms of distortion of an octahedron. The tetragonal distortion (symmetrical distortion along one C_4 axis) gives D_{4h} symmetry, the rhombic distortion (unsymmetrical distortion along one C_4 axis) gives D_{2h} symmetry and the trigonal distortion gives D_{3d} symmetry. The tetragonal distortion mostcommonly involves an elongation of one C_4 axis and in the limit two trans ligands are lost completely, leaving a square planar 4-coordinate complex.

Octahedral

Limitations of VBT

- A number of assumption are involved

- Quantitative interpretations of magnetic data is not given

- The exhibition of color by coordination compound is not explained

- Weak and strong ligand cannot be distinguished

- Whether the complex of coordination 4 is tetrahedral or square planer are not predicted exactly

- The thermodynamic and kinetic stabilities of coordination compounds are not quantitatively predicted

Chapter 3

Study of Crystal Field Theory

Crystal Field Theory (CFT) Assumptions:

- The interactions between the metal ion and the ligands are purely electrostatic (ionic).

- The ligands are regarded as point charges.

- If the ligand is negatively charged: ion-ion interaction. If the ligand is neutral: ion-dipole interaction.

- The electrons on the metal are under repulsive from those on the ligands

- The electrons on metal occupy those d-orbitals farthest away from the direction of approach of ligands.

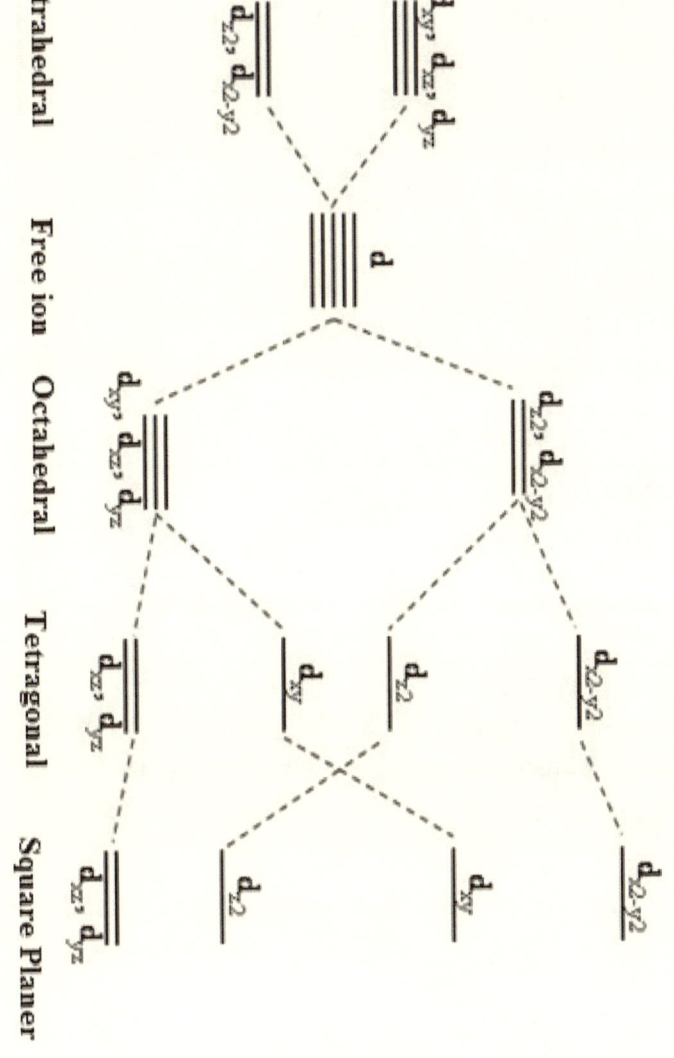

Splitting of d-orbitals in different fields

Crystal Field Splitting of d-orbitals

Crystal Field Stabilisation Energy (CFSE)

The crystal field stabilization energy (CFSE) is the energy by which the complex is stabilized relative to the free metal atom where there is no splitting of d orbitals. It can be calculated by:

$$CFSE = \{(n_{e_g} \times 3/5) - (n_{t_{2g}} \times 2/5)\}\, \Delta_0$$

where n_{eg} = number of electrons in e_g orbitals and nt_{2g} = number of electrons in t_{2g} orbitals.

For an octahedral complex, an electron in the more stable t2g subset is treated as contributing $-2/5\Delta$ whereas an electron in the higher energy eg subset contributes to a destabilisation of $+3/5\Delta$.

The final answer is then expressed as a multiple of the crystal field splitting parameter Δ (Delta).

Based on this, the Crystal Field Stabilisation Energies for d^0 to d^{10} configurations can then be used to calculate the Octahedral Site Preference Energies, which is defined as: OSPE = CFSE (oct) - CFSE (tet)

Note: the conversion between Δoct and Δtet used for these calculations is: $\Delta tet = \Delta oct * 4/9$

Consider the case of d^{10} ion where under the influence of an octahedral ligand field four electrons will move to higher energy e_g orbitals and six electrons to lower energy t_{2g} orbitals. Thus, the result for d^{10} system (eg. $Zn^{2+)}$ is no change in energy.

CFSE = {(4 x 3/5)–(6 x 2/5)}$\Delta 0$ = 0

A similar result would be obtained for a d^0 (e.g. Sc^{3+}) and a d^5 (e.g. Mn^{2+}, Fe^{3+}) electron configuration. In other words such ions would not be affected by the field of the ligands. Let us consider the other cases.

Taking for example $[Ti(H_2O)_6]^{3+}$ in which metal ion has d^1 configuration the CFSE is -0.4Δo.

Similarly for d^2 configuration ($[V(H_2O)_6]^{3+}$ the CFSE is -0.8Δo and in d^3 (Cr^{3+}) and d^8 (Ni^{2+}) it will be – 1.2Δo.

Cystal Field Stabilisation Energies (CFSE) and Octahedral Site Preference Energies (OSPE)

Total d-electrons	Octahedral		Tetrahedral		OSPE
	configuration	CFSE	configuration	CFSE	
d^0	t_{2g}^0	$0\ \Delta o$	e^0	$0\ \Delta t$	$0\ \Delta o$
d^1	t_{2g}^1	$-2/5\ \Delta o$	e^1	$-3/5\ \Delta t$	$-6/45\ \Delta o$
d^2	t_{2g}^2	$-4/5\ \Delta o$	e^2	$-6/5\ \Delta t$	$-12/45\ \Delta o$
d^3	t_{2g}^3	$-6/5\ \Delta o$	$e^2t_2^1$	$-4/5\ \Delta t$	$-38/45\ \Delta o$
d^4	$t_{2g}^3e_g^1$	$-3/5\ \Delta o$	$e^2t_2^2$	$-2/5\ \Delta t$	$-19/45\ \Delta o$
d^5	$t_{2g}^3e_g^2$	$0\ \Delta o$	$e^2t_2^3$	$0\ \Delta t$	$0\ \Delta o$
d^6	$t_{2g}^4e_g^2$	$-2/5\ \Delta o + P$	$e^3t_2^3$	$-3/5\ \Delta t + P$	$-6/45\ \Delta o$
d^7	$t_{2g}^5e_g^2$	$-4/5\ \Delta o + 2P$	$e^4t_2^3$	$-6/5\ \Delta t + 2P$	$-12/45\ \Delta o$
d^8	$t_{2g}^6e_g^2$	$-6/5\ \Delta o + 3P$	$e^4t_2^4$	$-4/5\ \Delta t + 3P$	$-38/45\ \Delta o$
d^9	$t_{2g}^6e_g^3$	$-3/5\ \Delta o + 4P$	$e^4t_2^5$	$-2/5\ \Delta t + 4P$	$-19/45\ \Delta o$
d^{10}	$t_{2g}^6e_g^4$	$0\ \Delta o$	$e^4t_2^6$	$0\ \Delta t$	$0\ \Delta o$

Crystal field stabilization energies for octahedral, tetrahedral, and square

System	Examples	Weak Field (High Spin)			Strong Field (Low Spin)		
		Oct.	Tet.	Square	Oct.	Tet.	Square
d_0	Ca_{2+}, Sc_{3+}	0	0	0	0	0	0
d_1	Ti_{3+} U_{4+}	0.4	0.27	0.51	0.4	0.27	0.57
d_2	Ti_{2+},V_{3+}	0.8	0.54	1.02	0.8	0.54	1.02
d_3	V_{2+}, Cr_{3+}	1.2	0.36	1.45	1.2	0.81	1.45
d_4	Cr_{2+},Mn_{3+}	0.6	0.18	1.22	1.6	1.08	1.96
d_5	Mn_{2+},Fe_{3+}, Os_{3+}	0	0	0	2.0	0.9	2.47
d_6	Fe_{2+},Co_{3+} ,Ir_{3+}	0.4	0.27	0.51	2.4	0.72	2.9
d_7	Co_{2+},Ni_{3+}, Rh_{2+}	0.8	0.54	1.02	1.8	0.54	2.67
d_8	Ni_{2+},Pd_{2+}, Pt_{2+}, Au_{3+}	1.2	0.36	1.45	1.2	0.36	2.44
d_9	Cu_{2+},Ag_{2+}	0.6	0.18	1.22	0.6	0.18	1.22
d_{10}	Cu_{+},Zn_{2+}, Cd_{2+}, Ag_{+},Hg_{2+}, Ga_{3+}	0	0	0	0	0	0

It can be assumed that the electrons added beyond d^3 will occupy eg orbitals in preference to pairing up in t_{2g} orbitals. This is not unreasonable, since there is a pairing energy (PE) associated with bringing electrons close to form a pair in an orbital. However, if the interaction between the metal ion and the ligands is sufficiently large so that $\Delta o > PE$, it becomes more energetically favorable for the fourth electron added to occupy a t_{2g} orbital.

Ligands which produce this effect are known as strong-field ligands and the complexes they form are called low-spin complexes. Whereas ligands for which $\Delta o < PE$, are known as weak-field ligands and they form high-spin complexes. Thus, when calculating the CESE of a strong-filed low-spin complex it is necessary to include the pairing energies associated with the additional electron pairs. In such cases CFSE for a low-spin complex (CFSEL) can be written as

$$CFSE_L = \{(n_{e_g} \times 3/5) - (n_{t_{2g}} \times 2/5)\} \Delta_0 + n(PE)$$

where,

n(PE) = number of additional electron pairs for a low-spin case.

It is important to note that that for a given metal ion the pairing energy (PE) is constant.

Thus, when the configuration is d^4, two cases arise: high-spin case and low-spin case:

(i) d^4 high spin case

This case arises when the ligands attached to the metal are weak field ligands. The electronic configuration of d orbitals in this case is $t_{2g}^3 e_g^1$ and the CFSE will be

28

$(3 \times -0.4\Delta o)+0.6\Delta o = -0.6\Delta o$

(ii)d^4 low spin case

This case arises when the ligands attached to the metal are strong field ligands. The electronic configuration of d orbitals in this case is t_{2g}^4 eg0 and the CFSE will be

$(4\times -0.4\Delta o) = -1.6\Delta o+ (PE)$

This case violates the Hund's rule.

The two cases differ in the number of unpaired electrons. The CFSE in the second case is higher than in the first case.

Similar situation can be observed in complexes of metal ions with d^5, d^6 and d^7 configurations. High- and low- spin gurations in an octahedral crystal field for d^6 (Fe^{2+})

Pairing energy, PE, depends mainly on the electronic distribution of the central metal ions and its value can be obtained from the atomic spectra of the elements. The Δo, which depends on metal ion, ligand and the geometry of the complex, is obtained from the electronic spectra of the complex. Consideration of the data related to PE and Δo for metal ions of d^4 to d^7 configurations that when $\Delta o>P$, low-spin complexes are formed and when $\Delta o<P$ then high-spin complexes are formed

Configuration	Ion	PE cm^{-1}	Ligand	Δ_0 cm^{-1}	Spin State Predicated	Observed
D^4	Cr^{2+}	23,500	6 H$_2$O	13,900	High	High
	Mn^{3+}	28,000	6 H$_2$O	21,000	High	High
D^5	Mn^{2+}	25,500	6 H$_2$O	7,800	High	High
	Fe^{3+}	30,000	6 H$_2$O	13,700	High	High
D^6	Fe^{2+}	17,600	6 H$_2$O	10,400	High	High
			6 CN$^-$	33,000	Low	Low
	Co^{3+}	21,000	6 F$^-$	13,000	High	High
			6 NH$_3$	23,000	Low	Low
D^7	Co^{2+}	22,500	6 H$_2$O	9,300	High	High

The CFSE for tetrahedral complexes and its comparison with the octahedral CFSE is given in below. The CFSE for d^0, d^5 and d^{10} configurations is zero in both octahedral and tetrahedral cases. In all other cases the octahedral CFSE is greater than that of tetrahedral CFSE. Overall octahedral complexes are more stable and more common than tetrahedral complexes, partly because of the formation of six bonds instead of four and also because of larger CFSE.

Tetrahedral complexes are favoured when:-

(i)   the ligands are large and bulky and could cause crowding in an octahedral complex,

(ii)   the ligands are weak field, so that the loss in CFSE is not that important,

(iii)   the central metal has a low oxidation state and as a result the magnitude of Δt is small, and

(iv)   the electronic configuration of the central metal is d^0, d^5 or d^{10} as there is no CFSE in these cases or d^1 or d^6 where the loss in CFSE is small.

d electron configuration	Arrangement of electrons		Spin only magnetic moment (in B.M.)	Tetrahedral CFSE(Δ_t)	Tetrahedral CFSE on octahedral CFSE scale ($\Delta_t = 4/9\ \Delta_o$)	Octahedral CFSE	
	e_g	t_{2g}				Weak field	Strong field
D^1		↑	1.73	-0.6	-0.27	-0.4	-0.4
D^2		↑ ↑	2.83	-1.2	-0.53	-0.8	-0.8
D^3		↑ ↑ ↑	3.87	-0.8	-0.36	-1.2	-1.2
D^4	↑	↑ ↑ ↑	4.90	-0.4	-0.18	-0.6	-1.6
D^5	↑ ↑	↑ ↑ ↑	5.92	0	0	0	-2.0
D^6	↑ ↑	↑↓ ↑ ↑	4.90	-0.6	-0.27	-0.4	-2.4
D^8	↑ ↑	↑↓ ↑↓ ↑↓	2.83	-0.8	-0.36	-1.2	-1.2
D^9	↑↓ ↑	↑↓ ↑↓ ↑↓	1.73	-0.4	-0.18	-0.6	-0.6
D^{10}	↑↓ ↑↓	↑↓ ↑↓ ↑↓	0	0	0	0	0

Electronic spectra of transition metal complexes

(i) d-d transition

In the electronic spectrum of a transition metal complex, d-d bands arise from electronic transitions which are largely localized on the metal ion. The magnitude of the energy gap Δo between the t_{2g} and e_g levels can be measured by recording UV – visible spectrum of the complex. The simplest example for a d-block element is presented by a d^1 ion such as Ti^{3+}.

Consider a complex like $[Ti(H_2O)_6]^{3+}$ which is violet in colour. In this the electron will occupy the orbital with the lowest energy that is one of the t_{2g} orbitals in the ground state of the complex. The next higher energy state available for the electron is the empty e_g orbitals.

If light of frequency υ, which is equal to $\Delta o/h$, where h is Planck's constant and Δo is the energy difference between the t_{2g} and e_g orbitals, strikes the solution, it should be possible for such an ion to capture a quantum of radiation to excite the electron from the t_{2g} to the e_g orbital (i.e., the change in configuration from $t_{2g}{}^1 e_g{}^0 \rightarrow t_{2g}{}^0 e_g{}^1$).

The absorption band that results from this process is found in the visible spectrum of the hexaaquotitanium(III) ion and is responsible for its violet colour.

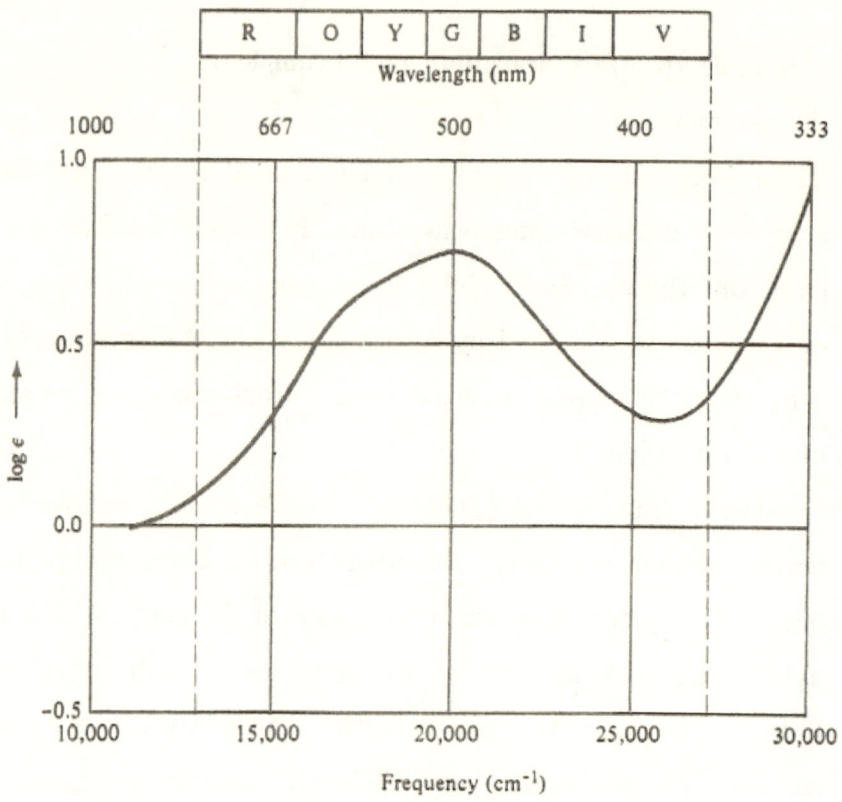

| R | O | Y | G | B | I | V |

Wavelength (nm)

Figure: The electronic absorption spectrum of $[Ti(H_2O)_6]^{3+}$

The position of the absorption band in the spectrum, its intensity and width are the three important features of the spectrum. The position of the absorption band (20,300 cm^{-1}) gives the value of Δo in $[Ti(H_2O)_6]^{3+}$.

Knowing that $1 kJmol^{-1} = 83.7$ cm^{-1}, the (20,300 cm^{-1}) value of Δo for this complex is $20300/83.7 = 243$ kJmol^{-1}.

The solution containing $[Ti(H_2O)_6]^{3+}$ absorbs yellow and green lights (which excite the d^1 electron from t_{2g} to e_g orbital) and thus transmits the complementary colour red-violet. Further, the single d

34

electron in this complex ion occupies an energy level 2/5 Δo below the average energy of d orbitals. Since the determined Δo value is 243 kJmol^{-1}, the CFSE comesout to be 2/3 x 243 = 97 kJmol^{-1}.

The maximum molor absorbance value (~5) indicates that the band is very weak. The molar absorbance values for one-electron theoretically "allowed" transitions are of the order of 10^4-10^5. This suggests that the d-d transitions (i.e. transitions between the same orbitals) are not "allowed" but "forbidden" according to the quantum theory. However, due to slight distortion in octahedral geometry (Jahn-Teller effect) and vibrations of the ligands which removes the centre of symmetry, the rigorous requirement is relaxed and, consequently low intensity broad bonds appear.

Appearance of d-d transitions in visible region is useful for quantitative determination of metal ions by spectrophotometric method. Broad shape of these bands minimize the chances of error in metal ion determination as slight wavelength variation in recording the absorbance will not have any significant effect.

In the case of tetrahedral compounds, the structures lack a centre of symmetry. As a result the d-d transitions become non-forbidden. Thus the tetrahedral complexes, in general, show considerably more intense d-d absorption bands than those of octahedral complexes; the increase in intensity is often by a factor of 10 or more. This explain why, for example, the pale red colour of the octahedral $[Co(H_2O)_6]^{2+}$ ion is changed by addition of Cl- ions to the intense blue colour of the tetrahedral $[CoCl_4]^{2-}$ ion.

(ii) *f-f* transition

The f elements have very distinct spectra caused by the electrons in the f levels. The electron configurations are determined in exactly the same manner as in the case of the d-complexes discussed above. However, the bands are of extremely low intensity, resulting in pale pastel colors for the salts and solutions of the lanthanides, the only case that we will consider. The f orbitals are very deeply buried in the interior of these atoms. Thus they are very little affected by any ligand crystal field effects. The absorption spectra therefore closely approximate the spectra of the same ions in the gas phase. Consider the example of Nd^{3+} for which detailed assignments of all the bands are presented in the figure at right.

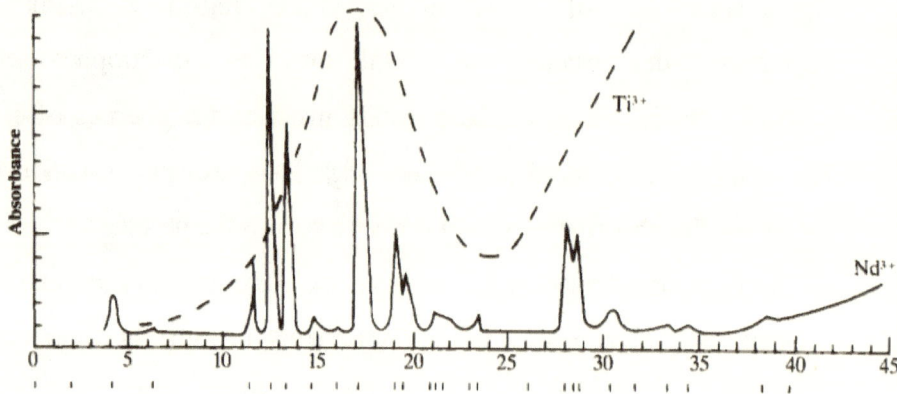

For the sake of comparison, the Ti^{3+} aqua ion d-d spectrum is superimposed using the dashed line.

CHARGE-TRANSFER COMPLEX

A charge-transfer complex (CT complex) or electron-donor-acceptor complex is an association of two or more molecules, or of different parts of one large molecule, in which a fraction of electronic charge is transferred between the molecular entities. The resulting electrostatic attraction provides a stabilizing force for the molecular complex. The source molecule from which the charge is transferred is called the electron donor and the receiving species is called the electron acceptor.

The nature of the attraction in a charge-transfer complex is not a stable chemical bond, and is thus much weaker than covalent forces. Many such complexes can undergo an electronic transition into an excited electronic state. The excitation energy of this transition occurs very frequently in the visible region of the electro-magnetic spectrum, which produces the characteristic intense color for these complexes. These optical absorption bands are often referred to as charge-transfer bands (CT bands). Optical spectroscopy is a powerful technique to characterize charge-transfer bands.

Charge-transfer complexes exist in many types of molecules, inorganic as well as organic, and in solids, liquids, and solutions. A well-known example is the complex formed by iodine when combined with starch, which exhibits an intense blue charge-transfer band.

In inorganic chemistry, most charge-transfer complexes involve electron transfer between metal atoms and ligands. The charge-transfer bands of transition metal complexes result from shift of charge density between molecular orbitals (MO) that are predominantly metal in character and those that are predominantly ligand in character. If the transfer occurs from the MO with ligand-like character to the metal-like one, the complex is called a ligand-to-metal charge-transfer (LMCT) complex. If the electronic charge shifts from the MO with metal-like character to the ligand-like one, the complex is called a metal-to-ligand charge-transfer (MLCT) complex. Thus, a MLCT results in oxidation of the metal center, whereas a LMCT results in the reduction of the metal center

Identification of CT bands

Charge-transfer complexes are identified by:-

- Color: The color of CT complexes is reflective of the relative energy balance resulting from the transfer of electronic charge from donor to acceptor.

- Solvatochromism: In solution, the transition energy and therefore the complex color varies with variation in solvent permittivity, indicating variations in shifts of electron density as a result of the transition. This distinguishes it from the π^* ← π transitions on the ligand.

- Intensity: CT absorptions bands are intense and often lie in the ultraviolet or visible portion of the spectrum. For inorganic complexes, the typical molar absorptivities, ε, are about 50000 L mol^{-1} cm^{-1}, that are three orders of magnitude higher than typical ε of 20 L mol^{-1} cm^{-1} or lower, for d-d transitions (transition from t_{2g} to e_g). This is because the CT transitions are spin-allowed and Laporte-allowed. However, d-d transitions are only spin-allowed; they are Laporte-forbidden.

charge-transfer complexes

Charge-transfer occurs often in inorganic ligand chemistry involving metals. Depending on the direction of charge transfer they are classified as either ligand-to-metal (LMCT) or metal-to-ligand (MLCT) charge transfer.

Ligand-to-metal charge transfer

LMCT complexes arise from transfer of electrons from MO with ligand-like character to those with metal-like character. This type of transfer is predominant if complexes have ligands with relatively high-energy lone pairs (example S or Se) or if the metal has low-lying empty orbitals. Many such complexes have metals in high oxidation states (even d^0). These conditions imply that the acceptor level is available and low in energy.

Consider a d^6 octahedral complex, such as $IrBr_6^{3-}$), whose t_{2g} levels are filled. As a consequence, an intense absorption is observed around 250 nm corresponding to a transition from ligand σ MO to the empty e_g MO. However, in $IrBr_6^{2-}$ that is a d^5 complex two absorptions, one near 600 nm and another near 270 nm, are observed. This is because two transitions are possible, one to t_{2g} (that can now accommodate one more electron) and another to e_g. The 600 nm band corresponds to transition to the t_{2g} MO and the 270 nm band to the e_g MO.

Charge transfer bands may also arise from transfer of electrons from nonbonding orbitals of the ligand to the e_g MO.

Trend of LMCT energies
Oxidation Number

$$+7 \ MnO_4^- < TcO_4^- < ReO_4^-$$

$$+6 \ CrO_4^{2-} < MoO_4^{2-} < WO_4^{2-}$$

$$+5 \ VO_4^{3-} < NbO_4^{3-} < TaO_4^{3-}$$

The energies of transitions correlate with the order of the electrochemical series. The metal ions that are most easily reduced correspond to the lowest energy transitions. The above trend is consistent with transfer of electrons from the ligand to the metal, thus resulting in a reduction of metal ions by the ligand.

Examples include:

1. MnO_4^- : The permanganate ion having tetrahedral geometry is intensely purple due to strong absorption involving charge

transfer from MO derived primarily from filled oxygen p orbitals to empty MO derived from manganese(VII).

2. CdS: The color of artist's pigment cadmium-yellow is due to transition from Cd^{2+} (5s) ← $S^{2-}(\pi)$.

3. HgS: it is red due to Hg^{2+} (6s) ← $S^{2-}(\pi)$ transition.

4. Fe Oxides: they are red and yellow due to transition from Fe (3d) ← $O^{2-}(\pi)$.

Metal-to-ligand charge transfer

Metal-to-ligand charge-transfer (MLCT) complexes arise from transfer of electrons from MO with metal-like character to those with ligand-like character.[1][4] This is most commonly observed in complexes with ligands having low-lying π^* orbitals, especially aromatic ligands. The transition will occur at low energy if the metal ion has a low oxidation number, for its d orbitals will relatively be high in energy.

Examples of such ligands taking part in MLCT include 2,2'-bipyridine (bipy), 1,10-phenanthroline (phen), CO, CN⁻ and SCN⁻. Examples of these complexes include:

1. Tris(2,2'-bipyridyl)ruthenium(II) : This orange-color complex is being studied,[5] as the excited state resulting from this charge transfer has a lifetime of microseconds and the complex is a versatile photochemical redox reagent.

2. W(CO)₄(phen)

41

3. $Fe(CO)_3(bipy)$

Photo-reactivity of MLCT excited states

The photoreactivity of MLCT complexes result from the nature of the oxidized metal and the reduced ligand. Though the states of traditional MLCT complexes like $Ru(bipy)_3^{2+}$ and $Re(bipy)(CO)_3Cl$ were intrinsically not reactive, several MLCT complexes that are characterized by reactive MLCT states have been synthesized.

Vogler and Kunkely considered the MLCT complex to be an isomer of the ground state, which contains an oxidized metal and reduced ligand. Thus, various reactions like electrophilic attack and radical reactions on the reduced ligand, oxidative addition at the metal center due to the reduced ligand, and outer sphere charge-transfer reactions can be attributed to states arising from MLCT transitions. MLCT states' reactivity often depends on the oxidation of the metal. Subsequent processes include associative ligand substitution, exciplex formation, and cleavage of metal---metal bonds.

Color of charge-transfer complexes

Many metal complexes are colored due to d-d electronic transitions. Visible light of the correct wavelength is absorbed, promoting a lower d-electron to a higher excited state. This absorption of light causes color. These colors are usually quite faint, however. This is because of two selection rules:

The spin rule: $\Delta S = 0$

On promotion, the electron should not experience a change in spin. Electronic transitions that experience a change in spin are said to be spin-forbidden.

Laporte's rule: $\Delta l = \pm 1$

d-d transitions for complexes that have a center of symmetry are forbidden - symmetry-forbidden or Laporte-forbidden.

Charge-transfer complexes do not experience d-d transitions. Thus, these rules do not apply and, in general, the absorptions are very intense.

For example, the classic example of a charge-transfer complex is that between iodine and starch to form an intense purple color. This has widespread use as a rough screen for counterfeit currency. Unlike most paper, the paper used in US currency is not sized with starch. Thus, formation of this purple color on application of an iodine solution indicates a counterfeit.

Limitations of CFT

- The CFT ignores the attractive forces between the d- electrons of the metal ion and nuclear charge on the ligand atom. Therefore all properties are dependent upon the ligand orbital and their interactions with metal orbitals are not explained.

- In CFT model partial covalencey of metal-ligand bonds are not taken into consideration. According to CFT metal–ligands bonding is purely electrostatic. Which is not so true?

- In CFT only d- electrons of the metal ion are considerd the other orbitals such as s, px, py, pz are not taken into consideration.

- In CFT π orbitals of ligand are not considerd.

- CFT mainly affected by spectra chemical series , which is as below:

  I- < Br- < Cl- < F- < OH- < H2O < NH3 < CO etc.

  a. As a ligand are assumed to be point charges, it is expected that the ionic ligand should have greater splitting effect. However actually they found to be at lower end of the spectrochemical series.

  b. Though OH⁻ in the spectrochemical series lies below H2O and NH_3 , yet it produces greater splitting effect.

  c. CFT is unable to explain the relative strength of ligands.

- CFT gave no information about π bond formation in ligand.

- CFT don't explain the effect of π bond on $\Delta 0$.

Jahn Teller Theorem

The Jahn-Teller Theorem (named after Hermann Arthur Jahn and Edward Teller), was published in 1937 and essentially means that:

In a nonlinear molecule, if degenerate orbitals are asymmetrically occupied, a distortion will occur to remove the degeneracy.

(or)

In an electronically degenerate state, a nonlinear molecule undergoes distortion to remove the degeneracy by lowering the symmetry and thus by lowering the energy.

Jahn Teller Distortion types

e- No	1	2	3	4	5	6	7	8	9	10
HS	w	w	-	s	-	w	w	-	s	-
LS	w	w	-	w	w	-	s	-	s	-

w: weak Jahn–Teller effect (t2g orbitals unevenly occupied)

s: strong Jahn–Teller effect expected (eg orbitals unevenly occupied)

Blank: no Jahn–Teller effect expected

Chapter 4

Study of Ligand Field Theory

The valence-bond model and the crystal field theory explain some aspects of the chemistry of the transition metals, but neither model is good at predicting all of the properties of transition-metal complexes. A third model, based on molecular orbital theory, was therefore developed that is known as ligand-field theory. Ligand-field theory is more powerful than either the valence-bond or crystal-field theories.

For instance the metal-ligand charge transfer (MLCT), being hard to explain by regarding the ligands as negative point charges, is now regarded in light of possible metal-ligand orbital overlaps and thus more conceptually feasible for LFT. LFT also describes the bonding in coordination complexes by regarding the metal d-orbitals and their energy levels relative to each other. The key idea is that orbitals with the same symmetry can overlap.

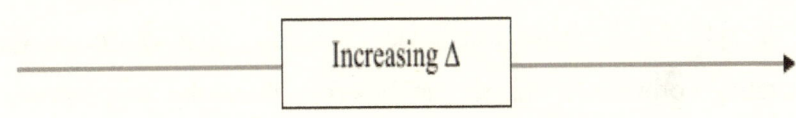

π donor < weak π donor < no π effect < π acceptor

For instance σ bonding is made up by an orbital overlap between ligand orbitals and metal ion orbitals with σ symmetry respective to the metal-ligand (M-L) bond axis. The classification of orbitals into σ, π and δ follows from the irreducible representation of the C∞v point group, where the bond axis contains the highest order rotation axis (C∞). Likewise, π bonding is made up by M-L π-orbital bonding overlap. A ligand with filled π-symmetry orbitals energetically similar to the metal π-symmetry dorbitals, would, if having no low energy. vacant πorbitals, donates electrons to these metal orbitals and creates a bond. This donation is depending on available empty or partly empty metal dπorbitals. The M-L bond is somewhat strengthened by this interaction, but the complementary antibonding MOs are typically comparable in energy to the σ anti-bonding MO. They are filled with electrons from the metal d-orbitals, when available, to become the HOMOs of the complex. For that reason, Δ decreases when ligand-to-metal π- bonding occurs. Oppositely, a πacceptor ligand has usually empty π-symmetry orbitals, typically vacant antibonding orbitals, lower in energy than metal π-symmetry dorbitals, available for occupation. One important π-bonding interaction in coordination complexes is the π-backbonding. This typically occurs when the ligand LUMOs are π^* orbitals and they couple with metal dπorbitals to form bonds. This is strengthening the metal-ligand bond and increasing the Δ. The corresponding antibonding orbitalsare higher in energy than the σ-antibonding orbital, and the ligands end up occupying their π^* orbitals and by that weakening the bond within themself.

Ligand Field Theory Assumptions

- One or more orbitals on the ligand overlap with one or more atomic orbitals on the metal.

- If the metal- and ligand-based orbitals have similar energies and compatible symmetries, a net interaction exists.

- The net interaction produces a new set of orbitals, one bonding and the other antibonding in nature. (An * indicates an orbital is antibonding.)

- Where no net interaction exists, the original atomic and olecular orbitals are unaffected and are nonbonding in nature as regards the metal-ligand interaction.

- Bonding and antibonding orbitals are of sigma (σ) or pi (π) character, depending upon whether the bonding or antibonding interaction lies along the line connecting the metal and the ligand. (Delta (δ) bonding is also possible, but it is unusual and is relatively weak.)

The ligand-field model for an octahedral transition-metal complex such as the $Co(NH_3)_6^{3+}$ ion assumes that the 3d, 4s, and 4p orbitals on the metal overlap with one orbital on each of the six ligands to form a total of 15 molecular orbitals, as shown in the figue below.

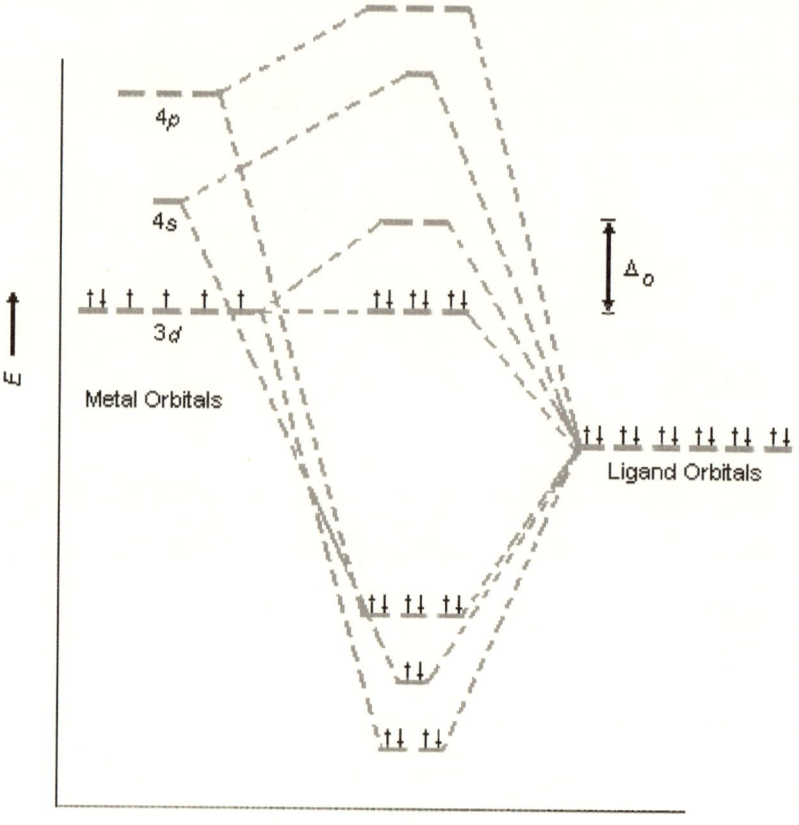

Six of these orbitals are bonding molecular orbitals, whose energies are much lower than those of the original atomic orbitals. Another six are antibonding molecular orbitals, whose energies are higher than those of the original atomic orbitals. Three are best described as nonbonding molecular orbitals, because they have essentially the same energy as the 3d atomic orbitals on the metal.

Ligand-field theory enables the 3d, 4s, and 4p orbitals on the metal to overlap with orbitals on the ligand to form the octahedral covalent bond skeleton that holds this complex together. At the same time, this model generates a set of five orbitals in the center of the diagram that are split into t_{2g} and e_g subshells, as predicted by the crystal-field theory. As a result, we don't have to worry about "inner-shell" versus "outer-shell" metal complexes. In effect, we can use the 3d orbitals in two different ways. We can use them to form the covalent bond skeleton and then use them again to form the orbitals that hold the electrons that were originally in the 3d orbitals of the transition metal.

Ligand Field Theory for Tetrahedral Complex

An example of a tetrahedral metal complex is VCl_4 which is shown in a convenient coordinate system. The 4s and 4p atomic orbitals of vanadium can be used to form sigma molecular orbitals. Although, the overlap patterns are rather complicated the 3dxz, 3dyz and 3dxy valence orbitals also are situated properly to form sigma molecular orbitals.

In terms of localized molecular orbitals both sd3 and sp3 hybrid orbitals are tetrahedrally oriented.

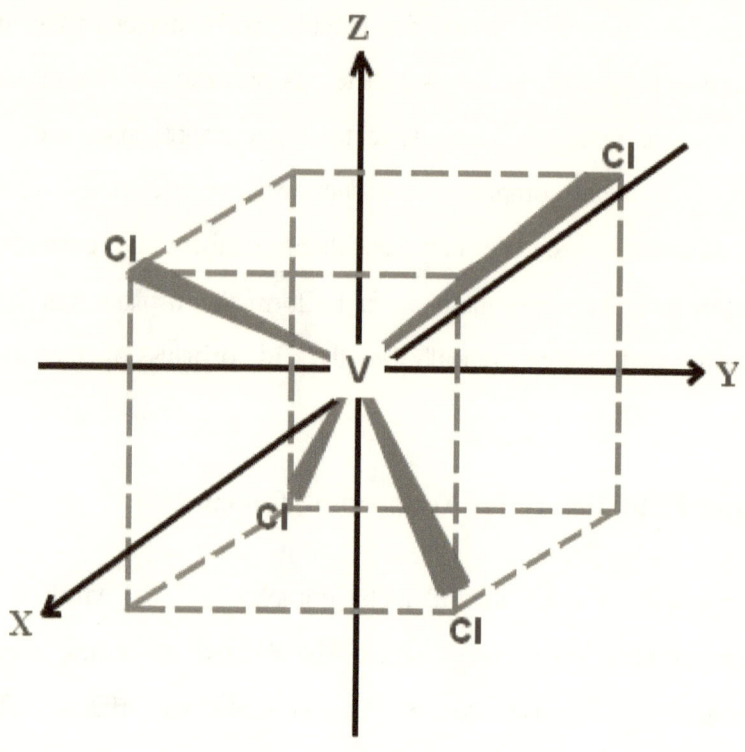

The ligand field splitting diagram for a tetrahedral complex such as VCl_4 is shown below.

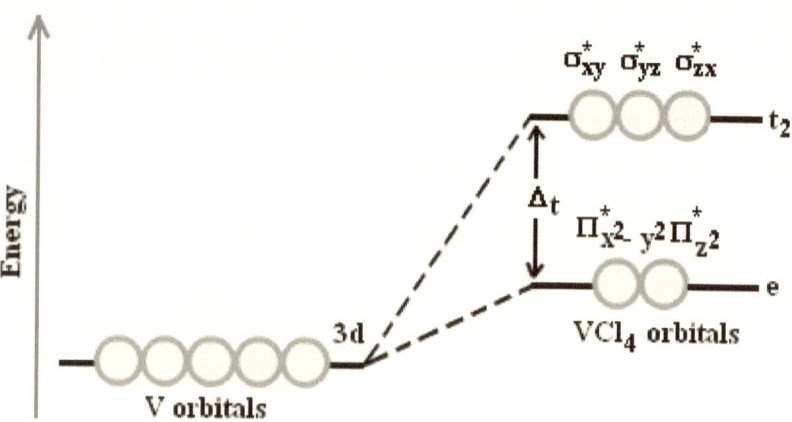

a. The anti bonding molecular orbitals derived from the 3d valence orbitals are divided into two sets.

b. The orbitals formed from the 3dxz, 3dyz and 3dxy orbitals are of higher energy than those formed from the 3dz2 and 3dx2-y2 orbitals.

c. Thus, the change from octahedral to tetrahedral geometry exactly reverses the role and the energies of the d valence orbitals of the central metal ion.

d. Δt is the energy difference between the t2 and e in tetrahedral complex.

e. From ligand field theory we can predict that the t2 orbitals in a tetrahedral complex will not form as strong sigma bonds with ligand sigma orbitals as will the eg octahedral orbitals thereby resulting in a much less energetic t2 level and a relatively small value.

f. Because of the small values all tetrahedral transition metal complexes have high spin ground state configurations.

Ligand Field Theory for Square Planar Complex

The d8 metal ions form square planar complexes. The example we will use here is [PtCl4]2-. The principle sigma bonding involves the overlap of 3p(sigma)Cl- orbitals with the 5dx2-y2, 6s, 6px and 6py metal valence orbitals. In the language of localized molecular orbital theory, the sigma bonding is summarized as dsp2 in a square planar complex.

Of principle interest the ligand field splitting of the anti bonding molecular orbitals derived from the metal d valence orbitals in a square planar complex.

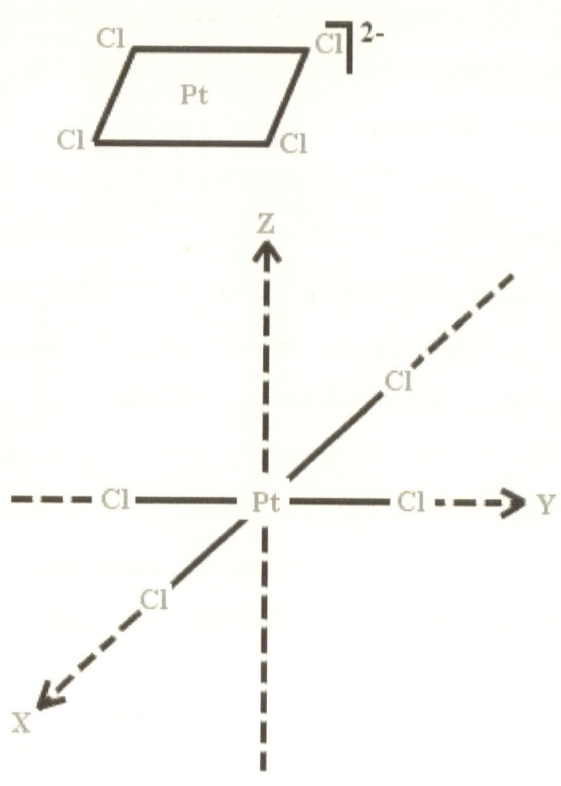

Square Planar Complexes

The ligand field splitting diagram for a square planar complex such as [Pt(Cl)4]2- is shown below.

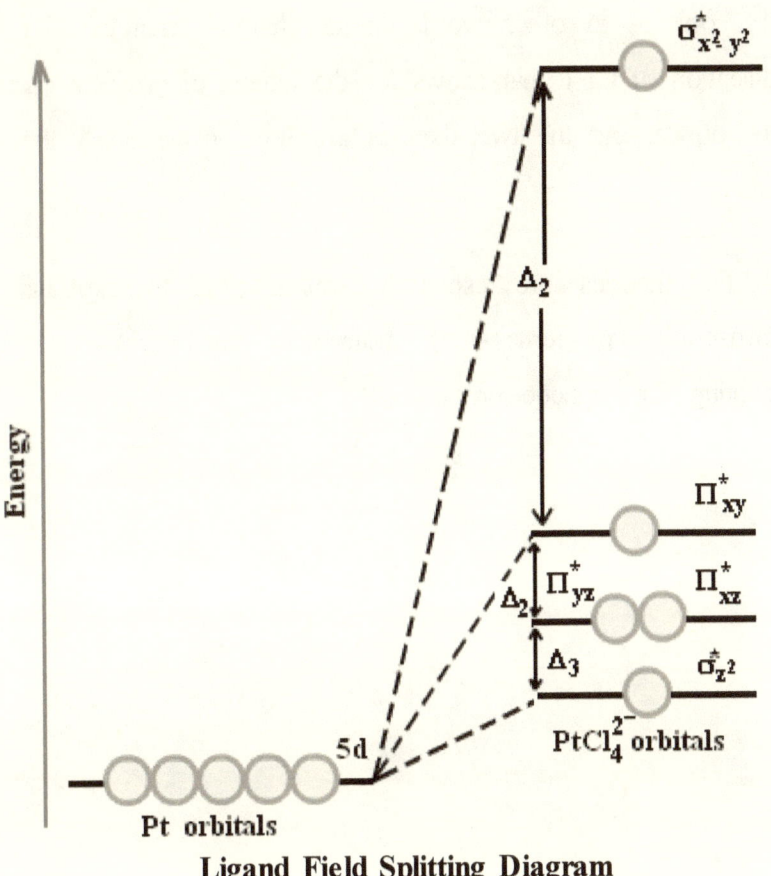

Ligand Field Splitting Diagram

The ligand field splitting in a square planar complex is rather complicated because there are four different energy levels. For all square planar complexes it is reasonable to place the strongly anti bonding orbital at the highest energy level.

CFT VS LFT

CFT assumes that bonds between the metal atom and the ligands are totally ionic – in other words, point charges whereas LFT is a modification of CFT that allows for the effects of covalent character in the bonds, but the two theories are used in essentially the same manner.

CFT/LFT theories are especially well-adapted to explaining the spectroscopic properties of transition metal complexes and accounting for magnetic properties

Chapter 5

Study of Molecular Orbital Theory

MOLECULAR ORBITAL THEORY

Molecular Orbital Theory (MO theory) is a method for determining molecular electronic structure by applying the orbital theory that holds for atoms onto molecules. In MO theory, electrons are not assigned to individual bonds, but are treated as moving under the influence of the nuclei in the whole molecule. In this theory each molecule has a set of molecular orbitals. It is assumed that the molecular orbital wave function ψj may be written as a simple weighted sum of the n constituent atomic orbitals χi, according to the following equation;

$$\psi_j = \sum_{i=1}^{n} c_{ij} \chi_i$$

where the Cij are coefficients that may be determined numerically, by substituting this equation into the Schrödinger equation and applying the variational principle.

A molecular orbital (MO) specifies the spatial distribution and energy of one or one pair of electrons, most commonly an MO is represented as a linear combination of atomic orbitals from the atoms comprising the molecule (the LCAO approach). For diatomics this is easily feasible, but for larger molecules this becomes increasingly complicated and is done by computers.

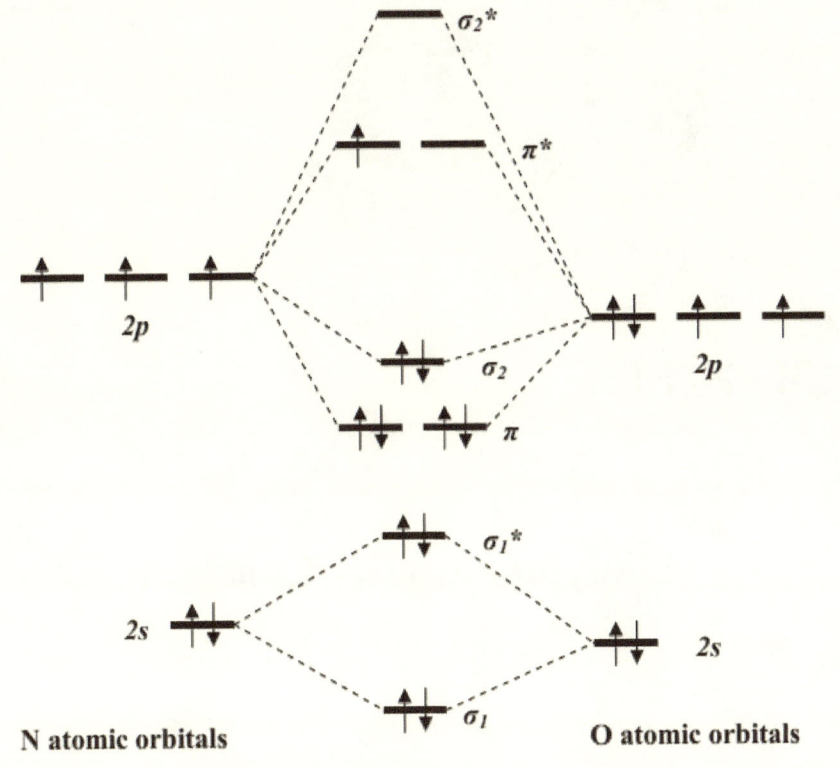

MO Digram for NO

Applied onto chemical problems, the MOs are divided into bonding orbitals, nonbonding orbitals and antibonding orbitals. The former represents a lower energy constellation than the parentage AOs, the latter a higher energy constellation. In principle molecules will form bonds if the atomic orbital MO combination becomes lower in energy than the AO combination. The qualitative MOmodel provides a simple description of bonding structures in molecules, and thus is a useful tool in applied computational chemistry.

CHAPTER 6

Study of Stability Constant

Stability of Co-Ordination Compounds

When the formation of complexes in solution is studied, two types of stabilities, thermodynamic stability and kinetic stability are considered.

In the language of thermodynamics, the equilibrium constants of a reaction are the measure of the heat released in the reaction and entropy change during reaction. The greater amount of heat evolved in the reaction, the most stable are the reaction products. Secondly, greater the increase in entropy during the reaction, greater is the stability of products. The kinetic stability of complexes refers to the speed with which transformation leading to the attainment of equilibrium will occur.

Determination of stability constant of complexes

In complexes the term stability is employed in two (1) thermodynamic stability and (ii) kinetic stability.

Thermodynamic stability deals with the bond energy, stability constant and redox potential. Thermodynamic stability refers to the change in energy on going from reactants to products, i.e., ΔG for

the reaction. Recall that $\Delta G = \Delta H - T\Delta S = -RT \ln K$, where ΔH is the enthalpy, ΔS the entropy and K is the equilibrium constant for the reaction

61

Kinetic stability deals with the rate of the reaction, mechanism of reaction, formation of intermediate complexes, and activation for the process etc. The thermodynamic stability of a species is a measure of the extent to which the species will form or be transformed into other species under certain conditions, when the system has reached equilibrium.

Let metal ion (Mn+) combines with ligand (L) to form complex MLn, then

$$M + nL \rightleftharpoons ML_n$$

$$K = \frac{[ML_n]}{[M][L]^n}$$

Thus by knowing the value of [M], [L] and [MLn] the value of K, stability constant of the complex MLn, can be computed.

The knowledge of stability constant is needed for computing quantitatively the concentration of free metal ion, ligand and any of its complexes formed in the system, under different conditions of pH. These data are extensively employed in analytical chemistry, stereochemistry, and biochemistry and in the technology of non ferrous and rare metals, solvent extraction, ion exchange etc.

There are so many techniques for the computation of stability constants:

1. Determination of stepwise stability constants by pH-metric method

As complexing processes are considered as occurring by a series of stages thus it is possible to express the formation (stability) constants referring specially to the addition of ligands in a stepwise manner as follows:

$$M + L \leftrightarrows ML \qquad K_1 = \frac{[ML]}{[M][L]} \qquad \therefore [ML] = K_1[M][L] \qquad (a)$$

$$ML + L \leftrightarrows ML_2 \qquad K_2 = \frac{[ML_2]}{[ML][L]} \qquad \therefore [ML_2] = K_2[ML][L] \qquad (b)$$

$$ML_2 + L \leftrightarrows ML_3 \qquad K_3 = \frac{[ML_3]}{[ML_2][L]} \qquad \therefore [ML_3] = K_3[ML_2][L] \qquad (c)$$

....

....

....

$$ML_{n-1} + L \leftrightarrows ML_n \qquad K_n = \frac{[ML_n]}{[ML_{n-1}][L]} \qquad \therefore [ML_n] = [ML_{n-1}][L] \qquad (n)$$

The constants K1, K2, K3,.........Knare called the stepwise stability constants.

The stepwise constants are related to the overall stability constant by the simple related:

$\beta_1 = K_1$

$\beta_2 = K_1.K_2$

$\beta_3 = K_1.K_2.K_3$

$\beta_4 = K_1.K_2.K_3.K_4$

Therefore $\beta_n = K_1.K_2.K_3. \ldots\ldots K_n$ \hfill (1)

A large number of techniques of great diversity are now being employed for the determination of stepwise stability constants. The most generally utilised and probably the most accurate and reliable method for the determination of stability constant is based on the potentiometric measurement of hydrogen ion concentration. This depends on the fact that pH of the solution is directly affected by complex formation, which is accompanied by the displacement of a proton from the acidic ligand. The magnitude of the observed pH change may be employed to determine the stability constant of the metal complexes by Bjerrum's method, Calvin and Wilson's method.

Out of these techniques Bjerrum's method is better as used by Calvin and Wilson. Bjerrum suggested certain formation functions such as $\bar{n}_A$, $\bar{n}$, pL. These functions are employed to calculate the stepwise stability constans.

The formation function ($\bar{n}$) of a metal ligand (M, L) system can be defined as:

$$\bar{n} = \frac{\text{Total concentration of L bound to M}}{\text{Total concentration of M}}$$

$$\bar{n} = \frac{[ML] + 2[ML_2] + 3[ML_3] + \ldots}{[M] + [ML] + [ML_2] + [ML_3] + \ldots} \tag{2}$$

Substitute the values of eq. (a), (b), (c) and (n) in (2)

$$\bar{n} = \frac{K_1[M][L] + 2K_2[ML][L] + 2K_3[ML_2][L] + \ldots}{[M] + K_1[M][L] + K_2[ML][L] + K_3[ML_2][L] + \ldots} \tag{3}$$

Now substitute the value of eq. (a) and (b) in (3)

$$\bar{n} = \frac{K_1[M][L] + 2K_1K_2[M][L]^2 + 3K_2K_3[ML][L]^2 + \ldots}{[M] + K_1[M][L] + K_1K_2[M][L]^2 + K_2K_3[ML][L]^2 + \ldots} \tag{4}$$

Now the value of eq. (a) substitute in (4)

$$\bar{n} = \frac{K_1[M][L] + 2K_1K_2[M][L]^2 + 3K_1K_2K_3[M][L]^3 + \ldots\ldots}{[M] + K_1[M][L] + K_1K_2[M][L]^2 + K_1K_2K_3[M][L]^3 + \ldots\ldots} \tag{5}$$

Now taking [M] common form eq. (5)

$$\bar{n} = \frac{K_1[L] + 2K_1K_2[L]^2 + 3K_1K_2K_3[L]^3 + \ldots\ldots}{1 + K_1[L] + K_1K_2[L]^2 + K_1K_2K_3[L]^3 + \ldots\ldots} \tag{6}$$

Now according to eq. (1) $\beta_n = K_1.K_2.K_3\ldots.K_n$, $\therefore$ bl $= K1$, $\beta_2 = K_1.K_2$, $\beta_3 = K_1.K_2.K_3$, and so on, substitute in the (6)

$$\bar{n} = \frac{\beta[L] + 2\beta[L]^2 + 3\beta[L]^3 + \ldots\ldots}{1 + \beta[L] + \beta[L]^2 + \beta[L]^3 + \ldots\ldots}$$

$$\bar{n} = \frac{\sum\limits_{i=0}^{n} i\beta_i[L]^i}{1 + \sum\limits_{i=0}^{n} \beta_i[L]^i} \tag{7}$$

$$\bar{n} = \sum\limits_{i=0}^{n} i(\bar{n} - 1)\beta_i[L]^i \tag{8}$$

In this same way for ligand-proton (L, H) system formation function $\bar{n}_A$ is defined as

$$\bar{n}_A = \frac{\text{Total concentrat ion of H bound to L}}{\text{Total concentrat ion of L not bound to M}}$$

$$\bar{n}_A = \frac{[HL] + 2[H_2L] + 3[H_3L] + \ldots\ldots}{[L] + [HL] + [H_2L] + [H_3L] + \ldots\ldots}$$

$$\bar{n}_A = \frac{K_1^H[H][L] + 2K_1^HK_2^H[H]^2[L] + 3K_1^HK_2^HK_3^H[H]^3[L] + \ldots\ldots}{[L] + K_1^H[H][L] + K_1^HK_2^H[H]^2[L] + K_1^HK_2^HK_3^H[H]^3[L] + \ldots\ldots}$$

$$\bar{n}_A = \frac{K_1^H [H] + 2K_1^H K_2^H [H]^2 + 3K_1^H K_2^H K_3^H [H]^3 + \ldots}{1 + K_1^H [H] + K_1^H K_2^H [H]^2 + K_1^H K_2^H K_3^H [H]^3 + \ldots}$$

$$\bar{n}_A = \frac{\beta_1^H [H] + 2\beta_2^H [H]^2 + 3\beta_3^H [H]^3 + \ldots}{1 + \beta_1^H [H] + \beta_2^H [H]^2 + \beta_3^H [H]^3 + \ldots}$$

$$\bar{n}_A = \frac{\sum_{i=0}^{n} i\beta_i^H [H]^i}{\sum_{i=0}^{n} \beta_i^H [H]^i} \tag{9}$$

Now formation function $\bar{n}$ is

$$\bar{n} = \frac{T_{CL^\circ} - \text{Concentration of L not bound to M}}{T_{CM^\circ}}$$

Where T_{CL° = Total concentration of ligand L and T_{CM° = Total concentration of metal M

$\therefore \bar{n} T_{CM^\circ} = T_{CL^\circ}$ - Concentration of L not bound to M

$\therefore$ Concentration of L not bound to M = $T_{CL^\circ} - \bar{n} T_{CM^\circ}$ \hfill (10)

From the value of $\bar{n}_A$,

Total concentration of L not bound to M = $[L](1 + \beta_1^H [H] + \beta_2^H [H]^2 + \beta_3^H [H]^3 + \ldots)$

$$M = [L] \sum_{i=0}^{n} \beta_i^H [H]^i \tag{11}$$

Substitute the value of eq. (11) in (10)

$$\therefore [L] \sum_{i=0}^{n} \beta_i^H [H]^i = T_{CL^\circ} - \bar{n} T_{CM^\circ}$$

$$\therefore [L] = \frac{T_{CL^\circ} - \bar{n} T_{CM^\circ}}{\sum_{i=0}^{n} \beta_i^H [H]^i}$$

$$\therefore \ [L]^{-1} = \frac{\sum_{i=0}^{n} \beta_i^H [H]^i}{T_{CL^-} - \bar{n}T_{CM^-}} \tag{12}$$

Taking log in eq. (12)

$$\log[L]^{-1} = \log_{10} \frac{\sum_{i=0}^{n} \beta_i^H [H]^i}{T_{CL^-} - \bar{n}T_{CM^-}}, \qquad\qquad \log[L]^{-1} = pL$$

$$\therefore \ pL = \log_{10} \frac{\sum_{i=0}^{n} \beta_i^H [H]^i}{T_{CL^-} - \bar{n}T_{CM^-}} \tag{13}$$

Calvin and Wilson have demonstrated that pH measurements made during titrations with alkali solution of ligand in the presence and absence of metal ion could be employed to calculate the formation functions $\bar{n}_A$, $\bar{n}$ and pL and stability constants can be computed. Irving and Rossotti[1], titrated following solutions against standard sodium hydroxide solution N° keeping total volume V° constant.

1. X mL mineral acid ($HClO_4$) E°
2. A + X_1 mL ligand
3. B + X_2 mL metal ion

On plotting the pH value of the solution with the addition of sodium hydroxide solution three graphs are achieved.

The formation functions $\bar{n}_A$, $\bar{n}$ and pL can be computed from the following eqations:

$$\bar{n}_A = Y - \frac{(V_1 - V_2)(N^\bullet - E^\bullet)}{(V^\bullet + V_1)T_{CL^-}} \tag{14}$$

$$\bar{n} = \frac{(V_3 - V_2)(N^\bullet + E^\bullet)}{(V^\bullet + V_1)(\bar{n}_A)(T_{CM^-})} \tag{15}$$

$$pL = \log_{10} \frac{1 + K_1^H[H] + K_1^H K_2^H[H]^2 + \ldots}{T_{CL^\circ} - \bar{n}T_{CM^\circ}} \times \frac{V^\circ + V_3}{V^\circ}$$

$$pL = \log_{10} \frac{\sum_{n=0}^{n} \beta_n^H \cdot \frac{1}{(anti \log B)^n}}{T_{CL^\circ} - \bar{n}T_{CM^\circ}} \times \frac{V^\circ + V_3}{V^\circ} \tag{16}$$

Where,

Y = number of dissociable protons

V_1, V_2 and V_3 = volume of alkali employed bring the solution 1, 2 and 3 to same pH value

T_{CL° = total concentration of the ligand

T_{CM° = total concentration of metal ion

By the knowledge of $\bar{n}_A$, $\bar{n}$, pH and pL protonation and stepwise stability constants can be computed by different methods such as:

Determination of stoichiometric stability constant

(1) Least square method

From Eqn (7)

$$\bar{n} = \frac{\sum_{i=0}^{n} i\beta_i[L]^i}{1 + \sum_{i=0}^{n} \beta_i[L]^i}$$

$$\text{For } i = 1; \quad \bar{n} = \frac{K_1[L]}{1 + K_1[L]} \quad \text{or} \quad K_1 = \frac{\bar{n}}{(1 - \bar{n})[L]} \tag{17}$$

$$\text{or } \log K_1 = \log \frac{\bar{n}}{1 - \bar{n}} + pL \tag{18}$$

$$\text{for } i = 2, \ \bar{n} = \frac{K_2[L] + 2K_1K_2[L]^2}{1 + K_1[L] + K_1K_2[L]}$$

$$\text{or } \frac{\bar{n}}{(\bar{n}-1)[L]} = \frac{(2-\bar{n})[L]K_1K_2}{(\bar{n}-1)} K_1 \tag{19}$$

$$\text{or } K_2 = \frac{1}{[L]} \cdot \frac{\bar{n} + (\bar{n}-1)K_1[L]}{(2-\bar{n})K_1[L]}$$

$$\text{or } \log K_2 = pL + \log \frac{\bar{n} + (\bar{n}-1)K_1[L]}{(2-\bar{n})K_1[L]} \tag{20}$$

The term $(\bar{n}-1)K_1[L]$ is negligible when $\bar{n} > 0.5$

$$\text{Hence, } \log K_2 = 2pL + \log \frac{\bar{n}}{(2-\bar{n})K_1} \tag{21}$$

The equations (18) and (20) are straight line equations. Thus by plotting different values of n and [L] straight line will be achieved. Thus the values of K1 and K2 can be computed.

(2) Half integral method / Interplotation at half $\bar{n}$ values

By putting the value $\bar{n} = 0.5$ in equation (18) we obtain

$$\log K_1 = pL$$

Similarly by putting the value $\bar{n} = 1.5$ in the equation (20) we obtain

$$\log K_2 = pL$$

It means if we plot a graph between $\bar{n}$ and pL then the corresponding values of pL at $\bar{n}$ equal to 0.5 and 1.5 gives $\log K_1$ and $\log K_2$ respectively.

In the same manner if $\bar{n}H$ is plotted against pH the values of $\log K_1^H$, $\log K_2^H$ etc. can be computed.

(3)　Linear plot method

Eq. (6) for $N = 2$ system may be written in form

$$yp_1 + xp_2 = 1$$

Where x and y are function of n and [L] and the parameter p_1 and p_2 are related to the stability constants. The six possible transformation of eq. (6) are

$$\frac{1-\bar{n}}{\bar{n}}\cdot[L]\cdot\beta_1+\frac{2-\bar{n}}{\bar{n}}\cdot[L]^2\cdot\beta_2=1 \tag{23}$$

$$\frac{\bar{n}}{(1-\bar{n})}\cdot\frac{1}{[L]}\cdot\frac{1}{\beta_2}+\frac{(\bar{n}-2)}{1-\bar{n}}\cdot[L]\cdot\beta_2/\beta_1=1 \tag{24}$$

$$\frac{\bar{n}}{(2-\bar{n})[L]^2}\cdot\frac{1}{\beta_2}+\frac{(\bar{n}-1)}{(2-\bar{n})[L]}\cdot\beta_1/\beta_2=1 \tag{25}$$

The other three transformations are obtained mearly be interchanging the values of x and y in the above equation. Eq. (22) can be rearranged as

$$y=-\frac{P_2}{P_1}x+\frac{1}{P_1} \tag{26}$$

Thus if y is plotted against x, a straight line of slope $-P_1/P_2$ and intercept $1/P$ should result.

(4) Point wise calculation method

Hearon and Gilbert have suggested the following methods for point wise calculation of K1 and K2.

Here β_2 = K1K2 is obtained graphically from a number of independent experiments. K1 is then calculated at several points using eq. (6) in the form of

$$K_1 = \frac{(2-\bar{n}).K_1K_2[L]^2 - \bar{n}}{(\bar{n}-1).[L]} \qquad (27)$$

And pointwise calculation of K_2 is made using the relation.

$$K_1K_2 = \frac{K_1[L] - \bar{n}(1 + K_1[L])}{(\bar{n}-2)[L]} \qquad (28)$$

Thermodynamic constants

The stability constants of the metal complexes are related to thermodynamic properties such as free energy charge (ΔG), enthalpy (ΔH) and entropy change (ΔS).

These values can be computed by usual equations:

$$\Delta G = -2.303 \, RT \log K \tag{29}$$

$$\Delta H = 2.303R \, \frac{T_2 T_1}{T_2 - T_1} \log \frac{K_2}{K_1} \tag{30}$$

$$\Delta S = \frac{(\Delta H - \Delta G)}{T} \tag{31}$$

Where, K_2 and K_1 are the stability constants at the absolute temperatures T_2 and T_1 respectively

Main Factors Affecting Stability of Complexes

The term stability may mean either thermodynamic or kinetic stability. In short if a complex is thermodynamically stable means it has large and positive free energy of reaction ΔG and if a complex is kinetically stable means it has large, and positive free energy of activation $\Delta G\#$

The main factors affecting stability of complexes are:

1. Charge on the metal ion

For a given ligand, greater the charge on the metal ion greater is the magnitude of crystal field splitting which ultimately affects the stability of the complex. A greater charge pulls ligands more strongly towards the metal, therefore influences the splitting of the energy levels more

Example,

Ions	Ligands	CFSE (Δ_o in cm^{-1})
V^{2+}	$6H_2O$	12600
V^{3+}	$6H_2O$	17700

2. Principal quantum number

Even though the metal ions have same charge, if the principal quantum numbers are different, then the magnitude of CFSE will be different and hence stability will be different.

Example,

Principal Q. No	Ions	Ligands	CFSE(Δo in cm^{-1})
	d6-Co^{3+}	$6H_2O$	18600
	d6-Rh^{3+}	$6H_2O$	20600

3. Nature of ligands

Properties of ligands like size, charge, dipole moment, polarizability and π-bonding capacity will affect the CFSE and stability of complexes. Smaller the size of the ligand, greater is the approach of the ligand with the metal ion and greater is the crystal field splitting.

Larger the charge on the anion, greater the polarizability and greater is the magnitude of crystal field splitting.

4. Chelation

Chelation increases stability. This is because the entropy factor is favorable in case of chelate complexes.

For example $[Cd(en)2]2+$ is more stable than $[Cd(MeNH2)4]2+$ since in the former there is chelation.

5. Macro cyclic ligands

The increased stability of complexes due to macro cyclic ligands is termed as "macro cyclic effect". The reason for this effect is mainly entropy and enthalpy factors. The macro cyclic ligands have cavities of particular size and hence selectively form strong complexes with metal ions of corresponding sizes.

For example, 18-crown-6 forms stronger complex with potassium ion than with sodium ion

6. Hardness and softness

Stability of complexes depends also on hardness and softness of the metal and the ligands. As per HSAB theory hard acids prefer hard bases and soft acids prefer soft bases.

For example, Ni^{2+} is a hard acid and hence it forms stable complex with NH_2 and not with soft ligand PH_3. But Pd^{2+} being soft acid forms stable complex with PH_3 rather than with NH_2.

7.   Surrounding conditions

Stability of complexes depends also on hardness and softness of the metal and the ligands. As per HSAB theory hard acids prefer hard bases and soft acids prefer soft bases.

For example, Ni^{2+} is a hard acid and hence it forms stable complex with NH_2 and not with soft ligand PH_3. But Pd^{2+} being soft acid forms stable complex with PH_3 rather than with NH_2.

Magnetic Properties of Coordination Complexes

Diamagnetic Compounds: Those, which tend to move out of a magnetic field. Example: N_2

Paramagnetic Compounds: Those, which tend to move into a magnetic field Example: O_2

The extent of paramagnetism is measured in terms of the magnetic moment, μ. The larger the magnitude of μ, greater the paramagnetism of the compound. Magnetic moment has contributions from spin and orbital angular momentum. A non-spherical environment may lead to quenching of the contribution from orbital angular momentum.

However, the spin-only magnetic moment survives in all cases and is related to the total number of unpaired electrons.

$$\mu_{eff} = \mu_{s.o} = 2\sqrt{S(S+1)} = \sqrt{n(n+2)} \ BM$$

Ion	# of unpaired electrons (n)	S	Predicted μ_{eff} values
Ti^{3+}	1	½	$\sqrt{3} = 1.73$
V^{3+}	2	1	$\sqrt{8} = 2.83$
Cr^{3+}	3	3/2	$\sqrt{15} = 3.87$
Mn^{3+}	4	2	$\sqrt{24} = 4.90$
Fe^{3+}	5	5/2	$\sqrt{35} = 5.92$

If there is a possibility for contribution from the orbital angular momentum

$$\mu = \sqrt{L(L+1) + 4S(S+1)}$$

For a given value of the orbital quantum number l, the magnetic quantum number m can have any values from $-l$ to $+l$ and L = sum of m

For d orbital electrons, $m = 2, 1, 0, -1, -2$
If there is only one electron in the d orbitals, L = 2

For an octahedral complex, orbital contributions are possible only when the t_{2g} orbitals are differentially occupied and for a tetrahedral complex the t_2 orbitals have to be differentially occupied.

Consider a Ni(II) complex, electronic configuration is d^8

For a free metal ion,

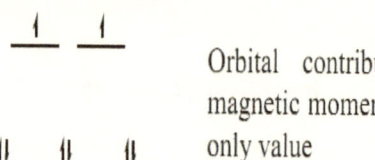

$$S = 1, L = 3 \text{ and } \mu = \sqrt{L(L+1) + 4S(S+1)} = 4.47 \text{ B.M.}$$

For an octahedral complex,

Orbital contribution is zero and magnetic moment is close to the spin only value

For a tetrahedral complex,

Magnetic moment is higher than the spin only value as there is positive orbital contribution

The effective (or resultant) magnetic moment of a substance is made up of two components:

i)   Contribution due to the orbital motion of the electron, and

ii) Contribution due to spin of the electron.

In case of transition metal ions the unpaired electrons are in the outer valence shell.   Due to strong ligand field the orbital motion of the transition metal ions in the complex is quenched and hence only the spin contribution is significant.

Magnetism deviation

Deviations are caused by two factors:

(a) orbital angular momentum (L) contributions to μ

1. In cases where orbital angular momentum is not quenched a somewhat more elaborate expression for μ applies:

$$\mu LS = [4S(S+1) + L(L+1)]1/2$$

which obviously simplifies to the μs expression if $L = 0$

If $L \neq 0$ then $\mu_{LS} > \mu_s$

Note: one special case: for a 6S ground state, $L = 0$ so μeff $= \mu_s$

2. orbital angular momentum is NOT quenched in degenerate ground states (especially T) so there is a significant contribution from L (egs. Co^{2+} and Co^{3+}, Fe^{2+} above)
3. non-degenerate ground states do not have a contribution from L so values close to the spin only moment are usually found (eg. Ni^{2+})

(b) contributions from spin-orbit coupling

1. Spin-orbit coupling means that S and L do not operate independently and J states need to be defined.

2. Since spin-orbit coupling is usually small for lighter transition metals, we can treat S and L independently (as was done in the earlier equation for μLS)
3. This isn't true for heavy metals and their magnetism is MUCH more complicated to predict

Temperature effects on μeff

Curie Law predicts μ should be T independent but that is often NOT the case:

1. orbital angular momentum and spin-orbit effects can come into play
2. magnetic moment is determined by the L and S contributions (plus spin-orbit effects) of ALL populated levels weighted by their populations so if other thermally accessible states exists, their population will change with T and so will their contribution
3. if there is any long range magnetic ordering (i.e. not behaving as isolated paramagnets) then μ will vary because these effects are T dependent.

Ferromagnetism: neighbouring spins align parallel with one another below a certain critical temperature (Tc Curie temperature)

- below Tc the material remains permanently spin aligned even when the field is removed
- field dependent effect

Antiferromagnetism: neighbouring spins align anti-parallel with one another below a certain critical temperature (T_N Néel temperature)

- below T_N the material tends to remain spin aligned and has a lower moment than expected
- common effect through bridging ligand due to 'super-exchange'

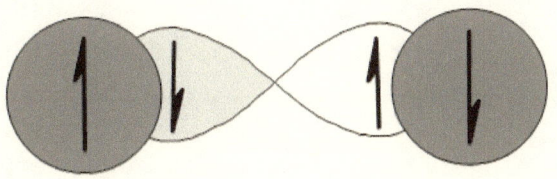

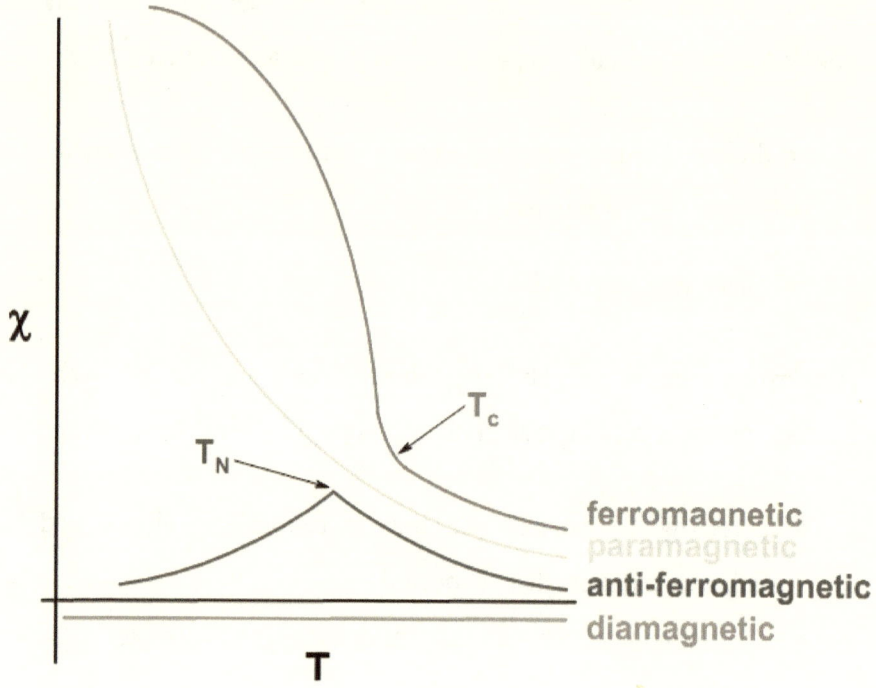

TRANS EFFECT

The Trans effect can be defined as the effect of a ligand over rate of substitution of another ligand positioned trans to it in the square planar complexes.

'T' is the trans directing group and 'Nu' is the nucleophilic ligand which preferentially substitutes the ligand 'X' which is trans to ligand 'T'.

* The Trans effect was first recognized by Ilya Ilich Chernyaev, a Russian chemist in square planar complexes of Platinum(II).

Difference between Trans influence and Trans effect

In general there are two factors contributing to trans direction of substitution as described below:

1) Trans influence: This is a thermodynamic factor. Some ligands weaken the M-L bond trans to them in the ground state and thus by facilitating the substitution.

E.g. Strong σ- donors like H⁻, I⁻, Me⁻, PR$_3$ etc., destabilize the M-L bond trans to themselves and thus by bringing the easy substitution of that ligand.

2) Trans effect: This is a kinetic factor and considered as true trans effect. It occurs by the stabilization of the transition state.

e.g. The strong π-acceptors like NO⁺, C$_2$H$_4$, CO, CN⁻ etc. stabilize the transition state by accepting electron density that the incoming nucleophilic ligand donates to the metal through π-interaction.

MECHANISM OF TRANS EFFECT

square pyrimidal   Trigonal bipyramidal

In the final compound, the incoming Nu occupies the trans position to ligand T.
Also observe the retention of configuration.

Starting from PtCl42−, the first NH$_3$ ligand is added to any of the four equivalent positions at random. However since Cl− has a larger trans effect than NH$_3$, the second NH$_3$ is added trans to a Cl− and therefore cis- to the first NH$_3$.

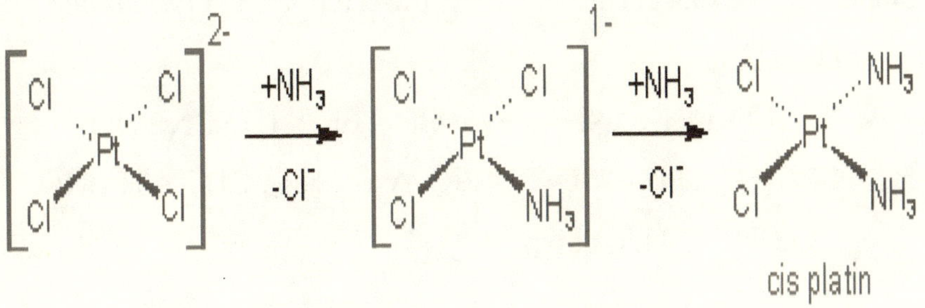

cis platin

If, on the other hand, one starts from Pt(NH3)42+, the trans product is obtained instead

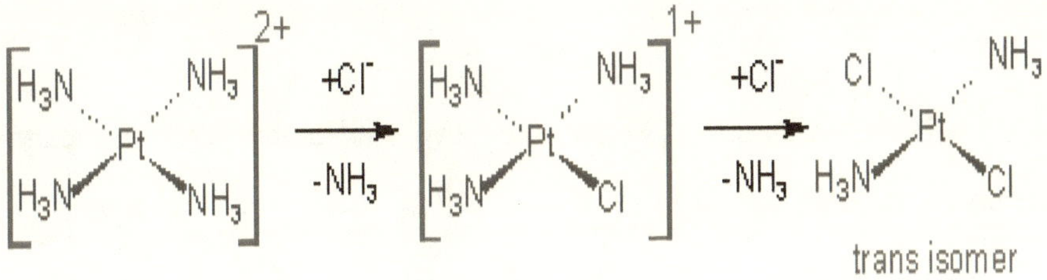

trans isomer

The Trans effect of a ligand may be due to:

a) destabilization of the trans M-L bond in the ground state (also called the trans influence) strong σ-donors (H-, PR3, I-, Meetc.) weaken the M-L bond trans to themselves

b) stabilization of the transition state (true trans effect) strong π-acceptors (eg. CO, C_2H_4, NO^+ etc.) remove electron density in the equatorial plane of 5-coordinate tbp transition states thus decreasing electrostatic repulsion.

Combining σ-and π- effects gives the observed Trans effect order: (Weak) to

$F^-, H_2O, OH^- < NH_3 < py < Cl^- < Br^- < I^-, SCN^-, NO_2^-,$

$SC(NH_2)_2, Ph^- < SO_3^{2-} < PR_3, AsR_3, SR_2, CH_3^- < H^-, NO,$

CO, CN^-, C_2H_4 (strong)

Kinetic Studies of Trans Effect

Kinetic studies: Most of the kinetic work is done on square planar Pt(II) complexes to monitor the trans effect during the substitution reactions.

* Both $\Delta S^{\ddagger}$ and $\Delta V^{\ddagger}$ are negative indicating the associative mechanism, either A or I_a.

Where:

$\Delta S^{\ddagger}$ = Entropy of activation

$\Delta V^{\ddagger}$ = Change in volume while forming the transition state from the reactants.

A negative $\Delta V^{\ddagger}$ corresponds to the transition state being compressed relative to the reactants. The volume of transition state is less than the combined volume of the reactants.

* The experimentally observed rate law for a square planar substitution reaction;

$ML_2TX + Nu \text{------>} ML_2TNu + X$

can be written as:

$$rate = k_1[ML_2TX] + k_2[ML_2TX][Nu]$$

Where:

T = trans directing ligand,

X = ligand positioned trans to T.

Nu = Nucleophile

The dependence of rate on the concentration of Nu indicates the associative mechanism.

* The stereo chemical retention of configuration is observed during substitution.

* In some cases the 5 or 6 coordinated species are isolated during the reaction.

www.ingramcontent.com/pod-product-compliance
Lightning Source LLC
Chambersburg PA
CBHW021547290526
45785CB00004BA/1944